Legal Research via
the Internet

The West Legal Studies Series

Your options keep growing with West Legal Studies

Each year our list continues to offer you more options for every area of the law to meet your course or on-the-job reference requirements. We now have over 140 titles from which to choose in the following areas:

Administrative Law	Family Law
Alternative Dispute Resolution	Federal Taxation
Bankruptcy	Intellectual Property
Business Organizations/Corporations	Introduction to Law
Civil Litigation and Procedure	Introduction to Paralegalism
CLA Exam Preparation	Law Office Management
Client Accounting	Law Office Procedures
Computer in the Law Office	Legal Research, Writing, and Analysis
Constitutional Law	Legal Terminology
Contract Law	Paralegal Employment
Criminal Law and Procedure	Real Estate Law
Document Preparation	Reference Materials
Environmental Law	Torts and Personal Injury Law
Ethics	Will, Trusts, and Estate Administration

You will find unparalleled, practical support

Each text is augmented by instructor and student supplements to ensure the best learning experience possible. We also offer custom publishing and other benefits such as West's Student Achievement Award. In addition, our sales representatives are ready to provide you with dependable service.

We want to hear from you

Our best contributions for improving the quality of our books and instructional materials is feedback from the people who use them. If you have a question, concern, or observation about any of our materials, or you have a product proposal or manuscript, we want to hear from you. Please contact your local representative or write us at the following address:

West Legal Studies, 3 Columbia Circle, P.O. Box 15015, Albany, NY 12212-5015

For additional information point your browser at

www.westlegalstudies.com

Legal Research via the Internet

Valerie J. Atkinson Brown

WEST

THOMSON LEARNING

Australia   Canada   Mexico   Singapore   Spain   United Kingdom   United States

WEST
——————✳——————™
THOMSON LEARNING

WEST LEGAL STUDIES

Legal Research via the Internet
by Valerie J. Atkinson Brown

Business Unit Director:
Susan L. Simpfenderfer

Executive Marketing Manager:
Donna J. Lewis

Executive Production Manager:
Wendy A. Troeger

Executive Editor:
Marlene McHugh Pratt

Channel Manager:
Wendy E. Mapstone

Production Editor:
Betty L. Dickson

Acquisitions Editor:
Joan M. Gill

Cover Design:
Dutton and Sherman Design

Editorial Assistant:
Lisa Flatley

For permission to use material from this text or product, contact us by
Tel   (800) 730-2214
Fax (800) 730-2215
www.thomsonrights.com

Library of Congress Cataloging-in-Publication Data
Brown, Valerie J. Atkinson.
   Legal research via the internet / Valerie J. Atkinson Brown.
      p. cm.
   "West Legal Studies series."
   Includes index.
   ISBN 0-8273-7450-X
   1. Legal research—United States—Computer network resources. 2. Internet. I. Title.

KF242.A1 B76 2001
340'.0285'4678—dc21   00-047699

NOTICE TO THE READER

Publisher does not warrant or guarantee any of the products described herein or perform any independent analysis in connection with any of the product information contained herein. Publisher does not assume, and expressly disclaims, any obligation to obtain and include information other than that provided to it by the manufacturer.

The reader is notified that this text is an educational tool, not a practice book. Since the law is in constant change, no rule or statement of law in this book should be relied upon for any service to any client. The reader should always refer to standard legal sources for the current rule or law. If legal advice or other expert assistance is required, the services of the appropriate professional should be sought.

The Publisher makes no representation or warranties of any kind, including but not limited to, the warranties of fitness for particular purpose or merchantability, nor are any such representations implied with respect to the material set forth herein, and the publisher takes no responsibility with respect to such material. The publisher shall not be liable for any special, consequential, or exemplary damages resulting, in whole or part, from the readers' use of, or reliance upon, this material.

$24.95 AGW 4811

Dedication

For my husband, Troy,
and in memory of Edna Lafferty,
my mother-in-law

Contents

**Chapter 5   Additional Resources on the
                Internet   75**

Acknowledgments

Much appreciation goes to Marlene Pratt, Betty Dickson, Janice Hoover, Brooke Graves, Lisa Flatley, and Chris Brock for being so professional and nice to work with. I would also like to thank Kenneth R. Thomson and Robert Christie for paying special attention to this project.

Thanks to many teachers, friends, classmates, and colleagues, past and present, for support and inspiration: Steve Head, Chris Walker, the Fry's, Charles Hodges, Alan Hamilton, Bill Hamner, Mildred and Vernon Atkinson, J.D. Van Atta, Chris Roscart, James Crisp, Gary Breaux, Stephen McNally, Clyde Lafferty, Wayne Gunter, Karen Kershaw, Steve Rouse, Nan Higgins, David Socha, Robert Ahr, Kevin Garrett, Frank Davis, III, Romie Szal, C.K. McFarland, Jay Farrington, Michael Burton, Pamela England, Joseph Schultz, David Garza, Tom Adelstein, Mike Landecker, Barry Burr, Federico Regaldo, Sebastian Van Haas, Peter Catellanos, Andrea Campbell, Mark Muldoon, Ron Yokubaitis, James Prappas, J.D. and Phil Savoy.

And a special thanks to the friendly folks at Upper Crust Bakery, Texspresso, and Bookpeople in Austin and The Coffee Pot in San Marcos where I spend endless hours reading, writing, and researching.

Thank you to KTSA's Cybercity host, Jack Landman, for promoting this project to Austin and San Antonio listeners. Appreciation goes to San Antonio Express News' initial online service, ENCONNECT. Jennifer Neal and Julie Weber of San Antonio Express News gave me the opportunity to showcase an Internet research booth at ITEC.

Thanks to Walter Prentice, J.D. for helpful suggestions about research sites and to Walter Wright, J.D. for excellent ideas about using the Internet as a classroom tool. And a big thanks to Hugh Jones, USPTO patent examiner and friend, for helpful updates about legal research websites.

And most of all, thanks to my best friend Prissi.

Introduction

Legal Research via the Internet is intended as a guide for attorneys, paralegals, law clerks, and law enforcement personnel who use the Internet as a serious research tool. Since 1993, the Internet has experienced massive growth. Part of that growth is in terms of users, because of new users learning to "surf the Net" and mine it for information. Another area of tremendous growth is Web-site development and home-page construction. The combined new traffic and new construction make today a confusing yet exciting time to take the plunge into Internet use.

Usually, after the initial "new toy" syndrome subsides, users feel a little baffled as to how to find what where. The Internet now plays a major role in legal and investigative research, as many sources of information (and clues for locating information) can be found online. There are also many excellent resources, reference tools, and lists of sites for legal research—but the what, where, and how are the focus of this book. By using this text, one can find specific sources to address specific questions and problems. This text takes the researcher to another level by providing step-by-step examples of legal research on current, "real-life" issues.

Legal Research via the Internet shows how to conduct research and collect information for weighing and presenting the strengths and weaknesses of clients' cases in memoranda of law.

To conduct effective and efficient Internet legal research, first you must learn how to:

- Identify important issues and distill them into words and phrases
- Organize and refine a search query
- Sort out search results

- Follow relevant leads and abandon unproductive lines of investigation quickly
- Document the queries performed (for future reference).

A systematic approach to conducting legal research through the Internet provides many benefits for your firm or solo practitioner supervisor. Research through the Internet:

- Saves time the next time you search
- Keeps a record for the client's file
- Provides records for subsequent cross-training of paralegals, law clerks, and attorneys.

The Internet itself is systematic, yet not necessarily organized. The researcher brings the organizational tools to the task. Blind searching yields little benefit, but if you develop good organizational tools and good research habits, your Internet legal research can be amazingly quick and productive. To create a method that works well for you, start with the following steps when conducting Internet research:

■ Research Steps

Step One

Fill out a search form, including all relevant information. Use a form established by your firm or create your own.

EXAMPLE Keep a research record by cutting and pasting relevant uniform resource locators (URLs) into a table.

Issues and Search Terms (words and phrases)		
Issues	*Case Law*	*Statutes*

Step Two

Formulate and refine your search query. Remember the Boolean connectors and keep a list of which ones are significant to and used with which search engines.

OR
AND [&]
NOT
BUT NOT

Make a list of words and phrases to use in your search (e.g.: "probable cause"). Then create a search-engine query checklist:

- Check spellings
- Check the effect of upper and lower case in the search syntax
- Try alternate terms.

Step Three

Select the search engines you want to try. Make some educated guesses as to which ones will lead to the most relevant information. Identify legal research sites that might be of use.

The connectors used in search engines vary, so become familiar with the characteristics of each. Keep a list of the connectors and syntax used by each search engine; your searches will go much faster than if you guess every time you have to do some research. Suggestions:

- For each search engine, print the help file or save it to a disk.
- Be aware of universal characteristics and symbols that can be used in a search.
- Know whether a search engine is case-sensitive.
- Determine if root expanders can be used.

The following search engines can become some of your best tools for Internet legal research:

Yahoo   <http://www.yahoo.com>
Alta Vista <http://www.altavista.com>
Google   <http://www.google.com> *or*
              <http://www.google.com/
               unclesam>
Mamma   <http://www.mamma.com>

Step Four

Document your query. You never know when you might need to refer back to it. Sometimes you forget the search terms you used and cannot produce similar results later. Though the Internet changes constantly, and identical search terms will produce slightly different results each time you use them, at least keep a record of how you searched. The difference will probably be only one or two URLs added to or subtracted from the initial list. If you do not keep a record (whether handwritten or electronic), you will have to start from scratch the next time—and will probably get completely different results.

Legal Research Form

The following is a general form that you can customize to your particular research needs:

Name _____

Date _____

Issue _____

Docket number (if assigned) _____

Interoffice file number _____

Deadline _____

Research Matrix

The following table is a sample of a basic matrix for recording your search plan and the results:

Search Engines	Primary Authority	Secondary Authority	Law Reviews, etc.

CHAPTER 1

Introduction to Legal Research

Chapter Outline

▓ The Legal Research Process

What Is Legal Research?

Legal research, which is conducted by a variety of individuals, companies, and institutions, is distinguishable from other types of research in that it is an entire process, not just factfinding. Legal research uses a process of legal reasoning, even though it is on a very small scale. For example, most law in the United States is based on court opinions, because the United States employs a common-law system of justice. No single, predefined set of rules applies to every problem. A myriad of rules and corresponding court interpretations exist. Court interpretation is what keeps the law continuously changing and evolving with society. For the most part, the law reflects societal changes. Each new and unique problem that confronts the courts must be dealt with on a case-by-case basis. *Legal Research via the Internet* shows you how to conduct research and collect information for presenting clients' strengths and weaknesses in memoranda of law.

Who Does Legal Research?

Legal researchers come from a variety of backgrounds. Generally, a person wanting to perform legal research is an attorney, law professor, paralegal, law clerk, or law librarian. Private investigators, law enforcement officials, writers, authors, and insurance company employees may also find themselves needing to do some kind of legal research. Though access to law libraries is often free, many people are not trained specifically to do legal research. For this reason, movements have arisen to demystify the law and make it less complex for the layperson.

How Is Legal Research Done?

A legal research problem or question might be one of the following types (among numerous others):

- Finding a state or federal statute
- Finding federal or state government documents
- Answering a basic legal question.

Traditionally, once a legal question was posed, the researcher began the search for an answer in the local public or law library. The researcher started at the card catalogue and moved on to the stacks to find relevant materials. Now, conducting Internet research from your office, library, or home can be a good alternative to traditional library and book research. We will begin our investigation of Internet legal research by looking at the steps outlined by most legal research guides on how to get started in solving a problem.

Legal research requires a formula for solving a problem. According to most established legal research guides, careful steps make the process go smoothly. These steps include:

- Identifying and analyzing facts
- Formulating legal issues
- Researching the issues
- Updating.

Identifying the facts requires making determinations as to the subject matter, the legal strategy, the relief sought, the parties, and the relationships between the parties, for example.

Formulating legal issues requires categorizing the legal problem at hand. The problem might be civil or criminal, on the federal, state, or municipal level. Each category may overlap with others; a given question may actually involve many complex, interwoven issues. For example, a divorce and a bankruptcy may affect one another. Separating each specific problem and identifying its impact on other problems and issues helps to solidify the tasks to be done in research.

Each issue, especially those affecting other issues, should be listed in a concise form. Outlines help some researchers, but are not necessary for others. However, any organizational tool, such as a flowchart or diagram, helps to document the research trail.

Once the issues have been identified, narrowed, and made concrete, sources for legal research are matched up with the problems needing research. A research form is a nearly indispensable tool for organization. As part of the documentation, the researcher must find and note all relevant constitutional provisions, statutes, administrative regulations, and case law.

The last step must not be neglected, that is, to check for any updates to the law.

The rule(s) applicable to a legal problem can be located in various ways. Lawyers traditionally rely on case law, statutes, digests, and treaties. Other typical legal research sources include:

- Decisions of appellate courts
- Executive decrees
- Regulations and rulings of administrative agencies
- Court rules, including the Federal Rules of Civil Procedure, Federal Rules of Criminal Procedure, Federal Rules of Appellate Procedure, and Federal Rules of Evidence; state and local rules may apply as well.

▓ Primary and Secondary Sources of Law

Primary Sources of Law

The United States Constitution

The United States Constitution is the ultimate authority regarding the law in this country. State constitutions and statutes, acts of Congress, and treaties cannot prevail over the federal Constitution. All courts, state and federal, are bound by it. The Constitution prohibits states from passing laws of certain types. The jurisdictions of the United States Congress and the federal courts are defined and outlined in the Constitution. States have jurisdiction over all other matters.

To determine where to start the research process, issues of state and/or federal jurisdiction must be decided. Federal matters include admiralty, customs, and interstate commerce. Marriage and divorce, real property, and wills are state matters.

The three branches of government (established by the Constitution) create primary sources of law through the passage of bills (statutory law), the promulgation of rules and regulations (administrative law), and the issuance of court decisions (common law or judge-made law). Laws and court opinions are officially published in the order they are issued. Thus, court opinions are collected in volumes by chronological order.

The Federal Register and the Code of Federal Regulations

The *Federal Register* publishes, and the Code of Federal Regulations codifies, administrative rules issued by federal agencies. Congress established the Office of the Federal Register in 1935 through the Federal Register Act. The Administrative Committee of the Federal Register maintains authority over the Federal Register system. The first issue of the *Federal Register* was March 14, 1936.

An amendment to the Federal Register Act (44 U.S.C. § 1510) created the Code of Federal Regulations (C.F.R.). This complies with the requirement that the Administrative Committee of the Federal Register have a publication that completely codifies agency documents.

The *Federal Register* contains information that does not appear in the Code of Federal Regulations. It includes repealed rules, adoption of new rules (policy statements), proposed rules, and agency organization and reorganization descriptions. The C.F.R. consists of more than 200 volumes published since 1938.

The *Federal Register* is accessible, through the National Archives and Records Administration, via the Internet at <http://www.access.gpo.gov/su_docs/aces/aces140.html> and <http://www.nara.gov/fedreg>.

Administrative Agency Publications

Administrative agencies have some quasi-judicial functions, in that they hold hearings and make decisions. Several private services publish and index these decisions, as well as rulemakings and other reports of agency actions, usually in looseleaf binders. A cumulative digest usually accompanies the looseleaf binders. Furthermore, each administrative agency may have publications of its own, either in print or online. As an example, the Environmental Protection Agency (EPA) site maintains links to administrative decisions.

FindLaw (<http://www.findlaw.com>) maintains links to many agency sites. Some of these agencies, such as the EPA, post decisions on their

Web sites. When users pull up a list of administrative agencies through a search on FindLaw
(<http://www.findlaw.com/01topics/
00administrative/gov_agencies.html>), they can
click on the agency of interest.

For example, clicking on "Environmental
Protection Agency" leads to a page (<http://www.
epa.gov/epahome/rules.html>) that has links to:

- "Regulations and Proposed Rules"
- "Codified Regulations"
- "Current Legislation"
- "Laws".

When you click on "Regulations and Proposed
Rules," you are led to <http://www.epa.gov/
epahome/rules.htm/#proposed>. Clicking on this
link leads you to the site for the Code of Federal
Regulations: <http://www.access.gpo.gov/nara/
cfr/index.html>.

Executive Documents

Executive documents are found in the *Weekly
Compilation of Presidential Documents.* "Orders and
Proclamations," printed in the *Federal Register,* can
also be found in the *United States Code Annotated*
and the *United States Code Service Advance.*

The United States Congress maintains a site
at <http://www.access.gpo.gov/congress/
cong005.html>. You can search for Senate, House,
and Executive Reports through this site. Instructions for searching the site appear at <http://www.
access.gpo.gov/su_docs/aces/aces180.html>, and
helpful hints for searching are given at <http://
www.access.gpo.gov/su_docs/aces/desc012.html>.

The Reporter Series

Court decisions at both the state and federal
levels are compiled chronologically, by date of
issuance, in volumes called *case reporters.* Each

level of the federal courts has at least one case reporter for its decisions. Decisions of state courts are collected in state case reporters. Each state has at least one official reporter for its highest court, and some states have more than one official reporter. Generally, the larger the state's population, the greater the number of reporters. Many state court opinions are also published in the West Group's *regional reporters,* which contain the full text of opinions of courts in a specific geographical region of the United States.

Advance sheets contain the most recent court decisions published in a given reporter series. These decisions are then included in the next binding of the appropriate reporter.

Federal Court Reporters

When federal issues are raised in state courts, the United States Supreme Court is the court of last resort. Any ruling made by the U.S. Supreme Court has profound importance in jurisprudential terms.

The official compilation of Supreme Court decisions is the *United States Reports.* An official citation to that reporter appears as [volume number] U.S. [page number]. The *United States Reports* started as a private venture in 1790 and became the official edition of Supreme Court decisions in 1817. Two other, private publishers also compile Supreme Court decisions: Lawyers Cooperative Publishing publishes the *United States Supreme Court Reports, Lawyers' Edition,* and West publishes the *Supreme Court Reporter.* A separate compilation of Supreme Court decisions, with synopses and headnotes, organized by subject, can be found in the *United States Supreme Court Digest.*

The *Federal Reporter,* which at first contained both circuit and district court decisions, was first issued in 1880. The *Federal Supplement,* published by West since 1932, took over publishing the decisions of the United States District Courts. After the inception of the *Federal Supplement,* the *Federal Reporter* restricted its coverage to the United States Courts of Appeal (circuit courts). These two reporters—the *Federal Reporter* and the *Federal Supplement*—also include decisions from specialized federal courts, such as the United States Court of International Trade.

State Court Reporters

State case reporters are part of the National Reporter System published by the West Group. The West Group also publishes a series of reporters called *regional reporters,* which provide the full text of opinions from courts in a specific geographical area.

State case law is slowly becoming available on the Internet. For example, California case law from 1934 to the present can be found through <http://www.findlaw.com>. At <http://www. findlaw.com/cacases>, you can search using:

- official citations and page numbers
- party names
- full text (using Boolean and proximity operators or wildcards)
- docket number.

Searching California cases requires registration through "My FindLaw."

Case law of other states, if available online at all, may be found through <http://www.findlaw.com/11stategov/index.html>.

Federal and State Statutes

Statutes at both the federal and state levels are collected in session laws and statutory codes. Session laws collect statutes in the order in which they were enacted. Statutory codes arrange those statutes according to subject matter. At the federal level, session laws are published in *Statutes at*

Large. The *United States Code* contains the codified version of the session laws. The *United States Code Annotated* and the *United States Code Service* are commercially published editions of federal statutes.

State session laws and statutory codes vary in organization and publishers. State statutes are published first as *slip laws,* then session laws, then as state codes. State codes resemble the *United States Code,* in that they are organized by subject matter; each state has at least one annotated code. State codes usually contain a detailed index. To supplement the volumes, quarterly pamphlets are issued and session law services provide more frequent updates. The state constitution can usually be found in the state code compilation.

Secondary Sources of Law

Secondary sources supplement primary sources in several ways. They serve to locate, update, develop, and interpret primary sources of law. Examples of secondary sources are treaties, hornbooks, Restatements, practice manuals, law reviews, legal encyclopedias, and the *American Law Reports Annotated.*

Any of the following have a variety of secondary authority resources:

- CataLaw: <http://www.catalaw.com>
- Law Crawler: <http://www.lawcrawler.findlaw.com>
- The LawEngine: <http://www.fastsearch.com/law/index.html>
- FindLaw: <http://www.findlaw.com>

Law Review Articles

Law review articles are written by both law students and experts with years of legal experience. They discuss trends in the law and the direction of those trends in specific areas of practice. Journal and law review articles may also discuss specific cases or present arguments for a specific interpretation or legal philosophy.

Many law reviews can be found, in whole or in part, on the Internet. One of the best sites for searching full text, back issues, and abstracts is at <http://www.jurist.law.pitt.eud/lawrev.htm>. The University Law Review Project also keeps researchers apprised of law review availability on the Internet: <http://www.lawreview.org>. For a list of full-text journals on the Internet, visit the Richmond Journal of Law and Technology site at <http://www.urich.edu/%7Ejolt/e-journals/ejournals.html/>.

American Law Reports

Selected state and federal cases also appear in the *American Law Reports* (ALR) published by Lawyers Cooperative Publishing Company. Each opinion selected for publication is followed by an *annotation* (a detailed analysis) of a specific point of law or fact situation raised in that case. ALR volumes contain about 20 cases each. *American Law Reports* covers issues that arose before 1969. Issues discussed in ALR range from petitions to change an adult's name to public utility responsibility for damages caused by a power outage.

Practice Manuals and Formbooks

Practice manuals contain forms and instructions on how to prepare those forms. They usually cover a specific area of the law. Formbooks tend to be generic and cover many areas of legal concern.

FindLaw maintains a page with links to forms at <http://www.findlaw.com/16forms/index.html>.

Legal Encyclopedias

American Jurisprudence 2d is one of the two best-known legal encyclopedias; the other is *Corpus Juris*

Secundum. Legal encyclopedias present summaries of hundreds of legal subjects, organized alphabetically. There are both a separate index volume and an index in each encyclopedia volume. Legal encyclopedias, which tend to focus on the historical perspective of a law or field of law, are a good starting point for research on topics with which you are unfamiliar.

The *Cornell Legal Research Encyclopedia,* developed by Cornell University law librarians, offers access to research guides and starting points. To access this guide, visit <http://www.lawschool. cornell.edu/library///Finding_the_Law/findlaw. html>.

▓ Citations

Every published case has a unique citation. Citations consist of:

case name (Plaintiff v. Defendant)
reporter volume number
reporter name
reporter page number
court that heard the case (location)
case year

Reporter names are abbreviated as follows:

U.S.	*United States Reports*
F.	*Federal Reporter*
F. Supp.	*Federal Supplement*
A.	*Atlantic Reporter*
N.E.	*North Eastern Reporter*
N.W.	*North Western Reporter*
P.	*Pacific Reporter*
S.E.	*South Eastern Reporter*
So.	*Southern Reporter*
S.W.	*South Western Reporter*

The Bluebook and Other Citation Authorities

The Bluebook, A Uniform System of Citation[1]
provides the rules for citing cases and legal materials. Citation formats for each state are outlined
in the *Bluebook,* as are federal and international
materials.

As the recognized standard for legal citation
form, the *Bluebook* is a bible of sorts to any law
student; one becomes familiar with it and uses it
throughout a legal career. Be aware, however,
that many states, courts, and other legal writers
use their own citation systems and abbreviations,
which sometimes vary significantly from those
in the *Bluebook.* With the changes in the online
world, it remains to be seen what citation methods
will be developed in the future and what reference
tool will emerge as the final authority.

Although the Harvard *Bluebook* has traditionally been the primary authority for citing legal
materials, other citation authorities are currently
emerging that supplement the *Bluebook,* including:

> Darby Dickerson, *ALWD Citation Manual: A
> Professional System of Citation* (Association
> of Legal Writing Directors/Aspen Law and
> Business, 2000)

> Alan L. Dworsky, *User's Guide to the Bluebook*
> (F.B. Rothman, 1991)

> C. Edward Good, *Citing and Typing the Law:
> A Guide to Legal Citation and Style,* 4th ed.
> (LEL Enterprises/Word Store Publications,
> 1997)

> C. Edward Good, *Legal Research—Without
> Losing Your Mind* (LEL Enterprises/Word
> Store Publications, 1997)

---

[1] *The Bluebook: A Uniform System of Citation,* 17th edition
(Cambridge, Mass.: Harvard Law Review Association,
2000).

Elaine C. Maier, *How to Prepare a Legal Citation* (Baron's Educational Series, 1996)

Mary Miles Prince, *Bieber's Dictionary of Legal Citations: Reference Guide for Attorneys, Legal Secretaries, Paralegals, and Law Students,* 5th ed. (William S. Hein & Co., 1997)

Larry L. Teply, *Legal Research and Citation,* 5th ed. (West Publishing/Wadsworth, 1999)

Citing and Typing the Law is particularly good at explaining information found in the *Bluebook* and in clarifying confusing points.

An alternate publication, the *ALWD Citation Manual: A Professional System of Citation,* can be ordered through Aspen Law and Business Publishers or amazon.com, or can be viewed and downloaded at the ALWD site (<**www.alwd.org/cm/index. html**>). The ALWD site, which is updated regularly, is of particular significance because of some variations from the prescribed *Bluebook* format. Here are some examples of varying abbreviations for case name citation:

Word/Term	*ALWD Citation Manual*	*Bluebook*
Administrator	Adminstr.	Adm'r
Advertising	Advert.	Adver.
Environment	Env.	Envt.
Regional	Regl.	Reg'l
University	U.	Univ.

"Introduction to Basic Legal Citation" can be found at <**http://www.law.cornell.edu/citation**>. The site is based on the sixteenth edition of the *Bluebook,* although the site will continue to provide updates and corresponding information about new editions.

Citators

Shepard's Citations is the recognized cross-indexing method used by the legal industry to find and cross-check documents. It provides the foundation for the researcher who wishes to obtain a history beyond the document at hand. The service gives cross-references and histories for case law for all 50 states, the District of Columbia, and Puerto Rico. In addition to statutes and court decisions, materials covered in cross-referencing include:

- administrative agency materials
- patents
- selected law reviews

A user can access Shepard's as a subscriber or on a pay-per-cite basis.

Case citators allow the researcher to cross-reference cited and citing materials, to trace case histories, and to check the validity of cases, statutes, and other law. Shepard's Citations lists published cases, statutes, regulations, constitutions, rules of court, legal periodical literature, and many other materials. Citators allow extensive cross-referencing, because every subsequent case that cited a particular case is listed beneath that first case. Shepard's citators allow the researcher to accomplish three tasks:

1. Find cross-referenced, subsequent cases, statutes, regulations, etc.
2. Check to see whether a source in question has been reversed, overruled, amended, superseded, etc.
3. Gather parallel citations and trace judicial histories.

Shepard's Citations are also available online, through LEXIS, WESTLAW, or the Matthew

Bender Web site
(<http://www.bender.com/bender/ open>). The
Matthew Bender staff analyzes each citing reference and compiles information into a comprehensive database.

▨ Introduction to the Internet

The Internet provides many resources to legal
professionals. After several years of substantial
growth and development, the Internet can lead
researchers to courts, cases, law review articles
and news sources. Refinements to these sites are
happening on a constant basis. Computers will
continue to make an indelible impact on the
practice of law. Networks and the Internet provide
the link to tools, but the researcher should always
be cognizant of changes and updates to search
engines and to the introduction of new tools to
expedite searching.

Internet History

In the summer of 1969, a group met to discuss
plans for a nationwide computer network. Later
that same year, a group sponsored by Bolt Beranek
and Newman, Inc., met for a reunion to discuss
the project titled ARPANET. The Department of
Defense's Advanced Research Project Agency
(ARPA) paid for the scientists' project.

The initial linking was to include four sites:
the Stanford Research Institute, UCLA, the University of California, and Santa Barbara. UCLA provided the first node. Devices called interface
message processors (IMPs) were built. The first
connection was a test between UCLA and a lab in
the Stanford Research Institute. By 1971, there
were more sites, including MIT and Harvard. By

1974, there were about 62. In 1981, there were at least 200. One of the key features of ARPANET was that its users were not necessarily programming or working on technical projects. Rather, simply sharing and transferring information with ease was the key to this new "invention," which was actually a collaborative project on which many scientists worked. Some, of course, played more important roles: Vint Cerf, for example, has been credited with much of the development of the Internet.

In a brief history of the Internet, Hobbes gave a sequence of events, by date, in the development of the Internet.[2] Though these events occurred later in the development of computers, they are undoubtedly the early phases of the new era of computerized information and information access. No longer are employees and households tied to "dumb" terminals. Citizens and employees are perfectly capable of dialing out and reaching points all over the world. In *The Internet Connection*, John Quarterman writes in terms of connectivity and points of access; his book also provides a very thorough treatment of Internet history and the demographics of Internet usage.[3]

The Internet provides gateway services (which are constantly developing) that enable one computer to interface with another. Database information available through the Internet expands daily. Users need know only one set of commands to communicate fully and effectively. The fact that a user does not have to learn many different sets of commands makes the Internet a universal tool. On the Internet, computer networks use a stan-

---

[2] See Valerie Atkinson, *Paralegal Guide to Intellectual Property* (Aspen Law and Business, 1994).

[3] John S. Quarterman and Smoot Carl-Mitchell, *The Internet Connection: System Connectivity and Configuration* (Addison-Wesley, 1994).

dardized computer language (*protocol*) to enable different computers to talk to each other. Transmission Control Protocol/Internet Protocol (TCP/IP) packages and addresses computer data in standard form. A user dials into an Internet provider that speaks TCP/IP. The Internet computer (*host*) receives signals sent via telephone or other transmission lines through a modem. A modem translates telephone signals into computer signals and vice versa.

Case Law Regarding the Internet

The Internet is not just a place to find and research case law; it has generated, and will continue to spawn, a good deal of litigation regarding its use and regulation. Jurisdiction, taxation, intellectual property (particularly in relation to trade names and copyright infringement), and many other fields of law are increasingly involved in Internet-based cases.

Complex jurisdictional issues arise in Internet-related cases perhaps more than any other area of law. In *Playboy Enterprises, Inc. v. Chuckleberry Publishing, Inc.*,[4] U.S. District Judge Shira Scheindlin held that a "Playmen" Web site violated a 15-year-old injunction against the sale, publication, or U.S. distribution of a magazine and related products. The judge also ordered the defendant, Chuckleberry Publishing, to refrain from allowing U.S. residents to subscribe to the "Playmen Pro" service.

Publishing on the Internet requires a new level of sensitivity and common sense about using trade names and trademarks. Before the widespread use of Internet communications, pirated publications in other countries could continue for years; now detection of piracy and knockoffs is swift. So

---

[4] No. 79 Civ. 3525 (S.D.N.Y. July 12, 1996).

are the consequences. Courts fully recognize the potential for dilution and confusion in the marketplace created by the Internet.

As one example, in *Giacalone v. Network Solutions, Inc.*,[5] Ty, Inc., a toy manufacturer, sought the right to use the domain name "ty.com". Computer consultant Philip Giacalone had used and registered that domain name before the toy company began using it. The judge enjoined Ty from interfering with Giacalone's use of the name. Ultimately, Ty presented a monetary settlement for use of the domain name "ty.com".

---

[5] No. C-96-20434 RPA/PVT (N.D. Cal., July 15, 1996).

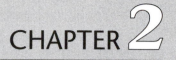

CHAPTER 2

The Internet as a Research Tool

Chapter Outline

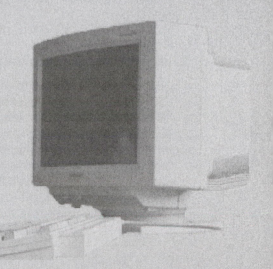

▓ Organizing Research Issues

Streamlining legal research requires the researcher to analyze facts. All facts should be organized into categories for maximum efficiency. For Internet research, several sites provide excellent leads to legal information. These include the Virtual Law Library (<**http://www.law.indiana. edu/ v-lib**>) and Cornell's Legal Information Institute (<**http://www.law.cornell.edu/index.html**>), among many others. Many commercial services also provide lists of links for research starting points. Several case scenarios in this text demonstrate legal research accomplished via the Internet (see Chapter 4: Internet Research Tasks).

Analyses

To organize a search, for any legal research problem, the researcher first makes a factual and legal analysis. The researcher then determines party or parties, subject matter, location and timing, applicable legal theories, relief sought, and procedural issues. The facts obtained from the client about the parties, subject matter, and timing determine the legal theories to be pursued, the relief to be sought, and the procedural issues that may arise.

Search Terms and Terminology

Initially, a researcher compiles a list of terms to be used to conduct research. Essentially, these are the same whether the research is done via books, commercial computer-assisted legal research services, or the Internet. However, the possibilities for research via bound books are limited to a predefined set of indexed terms. The freedom of computer-assisted legal research, in contrast, allows full document searches using terms of the researcher's choice. In essence, not only indexed terms can be used to find documents: *any* terms or combination of terms within the document can be used as the basis of a search.

After establishing the initial list of terms, a second, broader list can be used. This second list includes synonyms and related terms. Even terms abstractly related to the search are helpful, in that they may pull up documents that would otherwise not be found. Statsky's *Legal Thesaurus/Dictionary*[1] is an excellent resource for legal terms. The following paragraphs, excerpted from William Statsky's *Legal Research and Writing,*[2] show the importance of developing a systematic research process.

> Most people think that using an index is a relatively easy task—until they start trying to use indexes of law books! These indexes are often ... not comprehensive. To be comprehensive, an index might have to be as long as the text it is indexing. Hence, publishers are reluctant to include such indexes.

> Because of this reality, one of the most important skills in legal research is the creative use of indexes in law books. When you master this skill, 70 percent of the research battle is won. The CARTWHEEL is a word association technique designed to assist you in acquiring the skill. ...

> The objective of the CARTWHEEL can be simply stated: to develop the habits of phrasing every word involved in the client's problem *fifteen to twenty different ways!* When you go to the index (or to the table of contents ...) of a law book, you naturally begin looking up the words or phrases that you think should lead you to the relevant material in the book. If you do

---

[1] William P. Statsky, *Legal Thesaurus/Dictionary: A Resource for the Writer and the Computer Researcher* 627 (1985).

[2] William P. Statsky, *Legal Research and Writing: Some Starting Points,* 5th ed. (West Thomson Learning, 1999).

not find anything relevant to your problem, two conclusions are possible:

- There is nothing relevant in the law book.
- You looked up the wrong words in the index and table of contents.

Although the first conclusion is sometimes accurate, nine times out of ten the second conclusion is the reason you failed to find material that is relevant to the client's problem. The solution is to be able to phrase a word in as many different ways and in as many different contexts as possible. Hence, the CARTWHEEL.

* * *

If you applied the steps of the CARTWHEEL to the word *wedding,* here are some of the words and phrases that you would check:

1. *Broader words:* celebration, ceremony, rite, ritual, formality, festivity, etc.
2. *Narrower words:* civil wedding, church wedding, golden wedding, proxy wedding, sham wedding, shotgun marriage, etc.
3. *Synonyms:* marriage ceremony, nuptial, etc.
4. *Antonyms:* alienation, annulment, divorce, separation, legal separation, judicial separation, etc.
5. *Closely related words:* license, blood test, contract, minister, matrimony, marital, conjugal, domestic, husband, wife, bride, anniversary, custom, children, premarital, spouse, relationship, family, home, consummation, cohabitation, sexual relations, betrothal, wedlock, oath, community property, name change, domicile, residence, etc.
6A. *Terms of procedure:* action, suit, statute of limitations, complaint, discovery, defense, petition, jurisdiction, court, superior court, county court, etc.

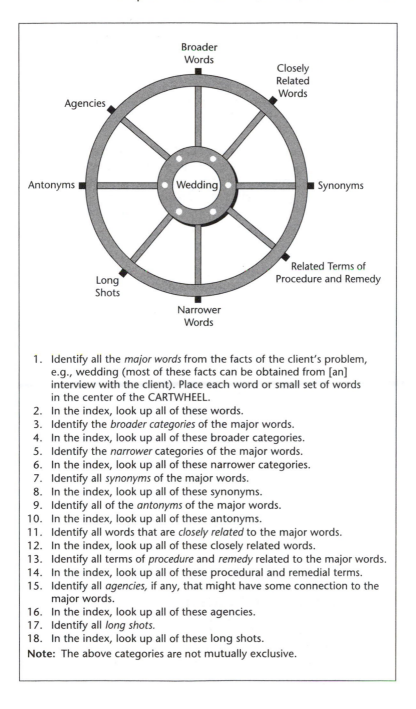

1. Identify all the *major words* from the facts of the client's problem, e.g., wedding (most of these facts can be obtained from [an] interview with the client). Place each word or small set of words in the center of the CARTWHEEL.
2. In the index, look up all of these words.
3. Identify the *broader categories* of the major words.
4. In the index, look up all of these broader categories.
5. Identify the *narrower* categories of the major words.
6. In the index, look up all of these narrower categories.
7. Identify all *synonyms* of the major words.
8. In the index, look up all of these synonyms.
9. Identify all of the *antonyms* of the major words.
10. In the index, look up all of these antonyms.
11. Identify all words that are *closely related* to the major words.
12. In the index, look up all of these closely related words.
13. Identify all terms of *procedure* and *remedy* related to the major words.
14. In the index, look up all of these procedural and remedial terms.
15. Identify all *agencies,* if any, that might have some connection to the major words.
16. In the index, look up all of these agencies.
17. Identify all *long shots.*
18. In the index, look up all of these long shots.

Note: The above categories are not mutually exclusive.

6B. *Terms of remedy:* damages, injunction, specific performance, divorce, partition, rescission, revocation, etc.

7. *Agencies:* Bureau of Vital Statistics, County Clerk, Department of Social Services, License Bureau, Secretary of State, Justice of the Peace, etc.

8. *Long shots:* dowry, common law, single, blood relationship, fraud, religion, illegitimate, remarriage, antenuptial, alimony, bigamy, pregnancy, gifts, chastity, impotence, incest, virginity, support, custody, consent, paternity, etc.

Law glossaries, dictionaries, and thesauri include word derivations, pronunciations, and citations to other sources. *Black's Law Dictionary* has been the standard for many years, but several other resources also provide helpful information regarding terms. Many of these same sources suggest an extensive range of terms for the researcher.

Preparing the Search

Preparing a search always requires careful planning and in most instances, planning and strategizing on paper helps. A custom-designed search strategy form helps to ensure orderly searching. Examine the legal problem at hand with an eye toward tactics, strategies for solving the problem, and the hoped-for results.

Strategies for Searching

Actual strategies for research include Boolean/thesaurus and non-Boolean, free-text searching. WESTLAW and LEXIS employ both Boolean and natural-language search methods.

Many Internet sites permit Boolean searching of documents.

When using databases and the Internet for legal research, it helps to know as many abbreviations as possible for words, titles, and names. This helps the researcher find documents that narrower searches might not locate. Pursuing variations in spelling also helps; sometimes the index terms entered into a site are inadvertently misspelled. A helpful text in this regard is *Communicating with Legal Databases: Terms and Abbreviations for Legal Researchers*.

To research a topic using keywords, try several techniques, using the CARTWHEEL strategies of broader words, narrower words, closely related words, antonyms, synonyms, long shots, or related procedural terms.

A helpful, short tutorial on how to conduct legal research, called "Finding the Law—Where to Start: Strategies for Legal Research," can be found at <http://www.lawschool.cornell.edu/lawlibrary/ Finding_the_Law/where_to_start/strategy.html>.

▓ Legal Research Skills for the Internet

In the past, legal research was based in manual research methods, that is, by using books and other print materials. Research today requires more sophisticated computer skills, including:

1. Understanding Boolean search operators
2. Knowing which database contains what information
3. Knowing how to download research results to a computer disk and how to manipulate the data found
4. Knowing how to import text found in a computer search into a document.

A systematic approach to the actual search process is detailed in the Introduction to this book. Using those research steps and strategies will make your search much more effective and efficient.

■ Search Engines

Search engines have their roots in search algorithms developed for mainframe computers. Some of these search tools include Lycos, Infoseek, Open Text, Yahoo!, Galaxy, Webcrawler, Alta Vista, Hotbot, Snap, Excite, Google, Mamma, and MetaCrawler. They provide a variety of ways to control your searches.

MetaCrawler, developed by Oren Etzioni, uses an intelligent querying system; with this tool, the user can specify phrases and is not limited to one-word searches. This takes at least one Internet search tool a step closer to the functions of commercial databases (such as LEXIS and WESTLAW) that have proprietary, ultra-sophisticated search engines.

Depending on the search engine, you can search for any search term, search for all search terms provided, or exclude certain terms. In addition to Boolean logic, you can use search engine math to refine your search queries. Search engine math allows you to add, subtract, or multiply search terms. To add, use "+"; to subtract, use "–"; to multiply, put your search terms within quotation marks. You can also use any combination of these symbols in one search.

Most major search engines provide features to assist researchers. For example, after submitting a search in Yahoo (<http://www.yahoo.com>), you can see if the result brings back a page with a list of terms for a "related search."

"Help" pages also make searching easier:

Alta Vista Help

<http://doc.altavista.com/help/search/
search_help.shtml>

Ask Jeeves

<http://www.askjeeves.com>

debriefing

<http://www.debriefing.com/>

Excite Help

<http://www.excite.com/info/searching.
html>

Find-It!

<http://www.itools.com/find-it>

Google Help

<http://www.google.com/help.html>

Hotbot Help

<http://www.hotbot.com/help/tips/
default.asp>

Lycos Help

<http://www.lycos.com/help>

Metacrawler

<http://www.metacrawler.com/
index_metafind.html>

Yahoo Help

<http://howto.yahoo.com/chapters/7/
1.html>

Lycos

Lycos, bought out by Spain-based Telefonica
in 2000, is an efficient search tool for finding topics on the Internet. Located through the World
Wide Web at <http://www.lycos.com>, this search

engine can pull up numerous items within a few seconds. Carnegie-Mellon University was associated with its development.

Yahoo

Yahoo (<http://www.yahoo.com>) is the most popular online guide to the Internet. Through Yahoo, one can search for information through a structured index or can perform a free-style search through a search tool (using keywords). *Yahoo* stands for Yet Another Hierarchical Officious Oracle. Yahoo's originators, Jerry Yang and David Filo, created Yahoo in April 1994 when they were Ph.D. students at Stanford's Electrical Engineering Program. They catalogued interesting sites on the Internet as merely a part-time project.

Meta-Search Engines

Some Internet tools, called *meta-search engines,* will submit the same query to many other search engines, sparing the researcher the trouble of entering it many times at many different sites. Helpful meta-search engines include:

- Find-It!, <http://www.itools.com/find-it>. Searches numerous search engines and compiles results.
- Dogpile, <http://www.dogpile.com>. Simultaneously searches many search engines; weeds out duplicates in search results.
- Mamma, <http://www.mamma.com>.
- All-in-One Search Page, <http://www.allonesearch.com>.
- Search-It-All, <http://www.search-it-all.com>.
- All4One Search Machine, <http://www.all4one.com>.

- Alphasearch,
  <http://www.alphasearch.org>.

An excellent site for search engine rules, <http://www.ijs.co.nz/snoozinf.htm>, includes an article on "Metasearch engines: Precision searching, reviews, and six rules."

Search Engines for Researching Substantive Law

Indexing tools such as Yahoo, AltaVista, or Webcrawler allow some streamlining of research queries, but problems arise when too many search terms are used. For example, a search for the "Tax Reform Act" pulls up more documents and listings than a search using "Tax Reform." The term "Act" adds extraneous documents to the list of search results. This is where some search engines fall short of the fine-tuned, sophisticated Boolean searches possible with commercial databases. Connectors and tools such as "and not" help a researcher avoid pulling up many extraneous documents, though "and not" is not truly Boolean.

In conducting a personal injury case search with a search engine such as Yahoo, the following terms could be used:

assumption of risk

personal injury

damages

negligence.

Next, elements specific to the case might be searched. After typing the terms into Yahoo, depending on the search results, one could use other search engines to supplement the search. Some legal-oriented search engines and mega-sites include:

- CataLaw,
  <http://www.catalaw.com>

- Law Crawler,
  <http://lawcrawler.findlaw.com>
- The Law Engine,
  <http://www.fastsearch.com/law/
  index.html>
- Meta-Index for U.S. Legal Research
  (provided by Georgia State University
  College of Law),
  <http://gsulaw.gsu.edu/metaindex>
- Legal Information Institute,
  <http://law.cornell.edu>
- Washlaw Web,
  <http://www.washlaw.edu/washlaw/
  washlaw.html>
- Emory Law Finder Electronic Reference
  Desk,
  <http://www.law.emory.edu/LAW/refdesk/
  toc.html>
- Guide to Legal Resources on the Web,
  <http://www.kentlaw.edu/clc/lrs/lawlinks>
- Hieros Gamos,
  <http://www.hg.org>
- Internet Law Library,
  <http://law.etext.org>
- World Wide Web Virtual Law Library,
  <http://www.law.indiana.edu/>
- Yahoo's Law Guide,
  <http://www.yahoo.com/government/Law>

Online help files assist in the research process.

▓ Listservs as a Research Tool

Listservs allow a researcher to receive a steady
stream of messages related to a particular subject. For example, a user interested in copyright
issues could access the Coalition for Networked

Information, <http://www.cni.org/Hforums/cni-copyright>, an excellent example of a listserv usable for legal research.

Any user may:

1. monitor ongoing dialogue
2. post a specific question or answer to another user who commented or asked a question
3. post a specific question or answer to all the listserv subscribers.

Listserv features are as follows:

- *Moderated*—has a moderator who manually reviews and approves each message.
- *Unmoderated*—no one reviews or approves messages before they are sent out to the group.
- *Subscriber-approved*—subscribers must be approved before they are permitted to join the listserv (be added to the list).
- *Open-subscription*—anyone can join the listserv, without the need for approval.

Although somewhat hit-or-miss in nature, listserv research is a "live" alternative to a World Wide Web site with links. They can be extremely useful for background research in a general area, for finding currently debated issues in a field, and for locating experts and advice regarding a specific problem.

Most listervs archive messages so that subscribers can refer to them at a later date. Listserv topics range from copyright of artwork to discussion of song lyrics to reprints of journal articles and papers. On any given listserv, discussions occur simultaneously and appear daily through email messages. The following actual email messages demonstrate one possible use of a listserv for legal research; the user broadcasts a query to all users or answers a question for another user. Note the variation in signature files appearing with each message.

- - - - - - - - - - Forwarded message - - - - - - - - - -

Date: Thu, 24 Oct 96 16:11:01 +1000
From: Timothy Arnold-Moore <tja@mds.rmit.edu.au>
To: Multiple recipients of list <cni-copyright@cni.org>
Subject: Re: fifty year rule

Jenny Hart wrote:

> My question relates to copyright in the estate of an author and comes from a colleague.
> An author of short stories died more than fifty years ago but in this particular collection it says copyright is with the Estate. My colleague wonders is it permissible to use an idea from one of these stories in a completely different setting and maybe different medium or does permission have to be obtained from the author's estate? Is it any different from taking a plot idea from one of Shakespeare's plays and using it in say a novel?
> How does the fifty year rule apply?

There are 3 aspects to this question.

1) Has copyright expired?

2) If not, is the use a breach of copyright?

3) Are there any other rights preventing me from using ideas and characters from this story?

Let's consider the first.

I'm not sure of the exact NZ situation but I think its the same as Australia. In Australia, if the short story had been published, performed in public, broadcast, or recorded and sold at the time of the author's death then 50 years after the end of the year in which the author died, the copyright expires.

If the short story was not published (or any of the other things) at the time of the author's death, copyright expires 50 years after the year in which the first of these things occurs (i.e. the Estate decides to publish them in some manner).

Otherwise the copyright NEVER expires.

2) If the copyright has expired, there is nothing that can be a breach of that copyright. If the copyright is still in force, then the use of ideas and/or characters from a story may or may not be a breach of copyright. I suggest you consult a lawyer in your jurisdiction to look at the material you are creating to see if it is likely to breach copyright.

3) It is possible that use of characters from a story may infringe trademark and related laws (particularly for some famous character like Peter Rabbit). These actions rely on the character having a reputation in the jurisdiction so obscure characters will probably not attract this protection.

Tim Arnold-Moore, LL.B. (Melb) | Multimedia Database
    Systems, RMIT |

tja@mds.rmit.edu.au B.Sc.(Hons Melb) | 723 Swanston St
- - - - - - - - - - - - - - - -

Tel: +61 3 9282 2487 Fax: ..2490 | Carlton 3053 | simul
    iustus
    http://www.mds.rmit.edu.au/People/Tja/tja.html | et
    peccator

- - - - - - - - - - Forwarded message - - - - - - - - - -

Date: Thu, 24 Oct 1996 11:27:51 +0930
From: Cathy Davis <cathy.davis@unisa.edu.au>
To: Multiple recipients of list <cni-copyright@cni.org>
Subject: Re: fifty year rule

Jenny

You asked:

> My question relates to copyright in the estate of an author and comes from a colleague. An author of short stories died more than fifty years ago but in this particular collection it says copyright is with the Estate.

You might need to check that the 50 year rule under New Zealand legislation. In Australia the 50 years after death only applies to works which have been published.

So if the short stories were not published during the author's lifetime, the clock didn't start ticking until publication occurred. Copyright remains in Unpublished work indefinitely.

An unpublished Shakespeare play would retain its copyright (but don't ask me who would own the rights now).

Cathy Davis

Record Management & Copyright Officer,
University of South Australia
cathy.davis@unisa.edu.au

Listservs help the user gather various pieces of information and put the information to use for other projects. Several law librarians maintain directories of listservs. Listservs provide a constant flow of information for the user who wishes to keep up to date without having to visit a multitude of sites on a regular basis. However, questions and answers to questions are random, and may not be on a topic of interest. A listserv is usually simply the email of a particular group of interested subscribers, with each response broadcasted to the whole user list. Private services, the larger data vendors (such as WESTLAW), and commercial providers offer clipping services that can be more narrowly targeted to areas of concern.

Listservs allow automatic and massive mail distribution and retrieval. One subscribes to a particular service of interest, then receives responses to general questions posted to the list. Each subscriber has an interest in the list topic area, and any user may be on several lists. Blatant advertising is not socially acceptable; as any experienced user knows, not following proper "Netiquette" will result not just in a slap on the wrist, but a massive flood of derogatory comments (usually called *flames*).

One question can elicit many responses from the listserv subscribers. The responses either point the user in the right direction (to other sites and resources) or provide direct answers to the questions.

Users who simply subscribe to the list may wish to review responses. Other users may be seeking information for immediate or future use. In this situation, the user should verify sources before relying on any answers to legal questions posted on a listserv.

Lloynette Louis-Jacques, librarian and lecturer in law at the University of Chicago Law School, maintains an excellent site on law listservs: <http://www.lib.uchicago.edu/~llou/lawlists/info.html>.

■ Newsgroups

With newsgroups, the user can "drop in" periodically to catch up on current developments, trends, and news in a particular topic area. The user does not have to subscribe and receive mail messages. For this reason, newsgroups have an advantage over listserv subscriptions, which can quickly fill up a mailbox.

■ Using the World Wide Web for Legal Research

To begin research, generally a World Wide Web (WWW) site is most effective. Provided the site is stable (that is, it is maintained and updated periodically and does not move sporadically), it can offer:

1. a good starting point for other research sites
2. daily updates
3. multimedia applications.

The Web, like the Internet, is designed to let users communicate with other users without seeing the machinery that makes the system work.

Ted Nelson coined the term *hypertext* in *Literary Machines 90.1*.[3] Hypertext provides the foundation for the abstract space known as the World Wide Web. In the words of the inventor, Tim Berner-Lee, these are the general concepts behind the World Wide Web:

> People who build a hypertext document of their shared understanding can refer to it at all times; people who join a project team can have access to a history of the team's activities, decisions, and so on; the work of the people who leave a team can be captured for future reference; and a team's operations, if placed on the web, can be machine-analyzed in a way that could not be done otherwise.[4]

The World Wide Web, a seamless web of information, allows the researcher to weave from one document to another. The best way to use the Web is to have a graphical interface or browser for searching, such as Netscape or Microsoft's Internet Explorer. Many older browsing and organizational tools for the World Wide Web have fallen by the wayside as more efficient and more widely distributed tools for navigating the Web have become available.

A sampling of World Wide Web home pages for a variety of services are found throughout the text. Each might contain an index or resource list, linked so that users only have to point-and-click on the listed resource to access the other site and its information.

---

[3] Ted Nelson, *Literary Machines 90.1* (Mindful Press 1990).

[4] Tim Berners-Lee, "WWW: Past, Present and Future," IEEE (Oct. 1996), at 77 (<http://www.w3.org/People/Berners-Lee>).

CHAPTER 3

Law on the Internet

Chapter Outline

■ Introduction

For classification purposes, the law is divided into two categories. *Substantive law* defines legal rights and duties to other people, entities, and the government. *Procedural law* is comprised of the rules that govern how the legal system operates.

Substantive law may be accessed at various sites on the Internet. This chapter introduces sites that allow access to substantive law documents.

■ Code of Federal Regulations

The Code of Federal Regulations (C.F.R.) is comprised of federal administrative rules, arranged by topic. The C.F.R. is easily accessed at <http:// law.house.gove/cfr.htm>, or at <http://www.law. cornell.edu/cfr>. Using the Cornell site, the C.F.R. can be searched by title and section, via the Government Printing Office search engine, by the Legal Information Institute's Index of Section Headings, or by the C.F.R. Table of Contents. Links to the most recent version of the C.F.R. are placed on the Internet by the Government Printing Office. The Cornell site contains the federal regulations in force as of specific revision dates that vary from title to title. The revision date for each title is shown in its table of contents.

Internet legal research allows a researcher to circumvent some, but not all, of the manual steps for research. Using the Internet, research can be conducted when searching for recent C.F.R. issues. Due to the sheer volume of historical issues of the *Federal Register* and C.F.R., only the past few years' worth of material has become available through Internet sites thus far.

■ Securities and Exchange Commission

One of the easiest and most efficient methods of obtaining SEC 10-K reports is to use the EDGAR (Electronic Data Gathering Analysis and Retrieval) database, found at **<http://www.sec.gov/edgarhp. htm>**. Once EDGAR is opened, click on "Search the Edgar Database." When the file opens, a box appears at the top of the page for typing in the name of a company. For example, if the researcher wants a 1995 10-K report for Coca-Cola, Inc., he or she would type "Coca Cola" in that box. When the company screen pops up, click on the 10-K report to open it.

■ FedWorld

FedWorld (**<http://www.fedworld.gov>**) leads to a variety of information. The subject categories are shown in the following home pages. This system can be thought of as a giant warehouse of government documents, studies, announcements, forms, and decisions. It is somewhat scattered, but as World Wide Web sites develop and become more streamlined, researchers should find more and more organization rather than chaotic searching.

The FedWorld main menu contains the following links:

Browse the FedWorld Information Network

Search Web Pages on the FedWorld
    Information Network

Search for U.S. Government Reports

Explore U.S. Government Web Sites

International Law

As opposed to a national legal system, international law lacks a formal, ultimate authority. Sources of international law include international organizations and conferences, international customs and traditions, and treaties between countries.

Researching international law involves searching the agreements and relations between nations. Examples are the General Agreement on Trade and Tariffs (GATT), <gopher://gopher.law.cornell. edu/00/foreign/fletcher/BH209.txt>; and the North American Free Trade Agreement. International treaties and conventions serve as the primary legal authority when there is a problem between two countries. International organizations that may become involved in disputes or agreements include the United Nations (<http://www.un.org>), the European Communities Court of Justice and Court of First Instance (<http://europa.eu.inf/cj/en/ index.html>), and the International Court of Justice (<http://www.icj-cij.org/>; mirror site, <http://www.lawschool.cornell.edu/library/ eijwww/>).

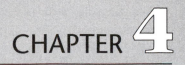
Internet
Research
Tasks

Chapter Outline

▓ Solving Research Problems

This section describes methods to solve a variety of research problems. Using several subject areas, these sample tasks show the different techniques for retrieving data and information. For each task, a research strategy outline helps the researcher organize the research. Each sample task explains the task and outlines obstacles to completing the task, information needed, records needed, and results required.

By using a research strategy note sheet, worksheet, or form, the researcher will have an organized plan laid out before logging onto the computer. Haphazard, hit-or-miss searching results in more time online and thus higher charges; organization of research before logging on minimizes costly online fees. Although some online services charge more than others, Internet service providers (ISPs) generally charge a flat monthly fee for unlimited access. These considerations determine which options are best for legal research. A researcher must weigh the cost of Internet online fees, commercial service fees, book subscription costs, and online legal information providers (such as WESTLAW) when planning a search strategy for maximum efficiency and best results.

▓ Internet Research Task Examples

Task #1: Tax Law

Incident

Rick and Nancy, who have been clients of your firm for more than 10 years, believe they overpaid their taxes, yet they are being audited. They want a representative with strong experience in working with the IRS.

Assignment

Tom, a firm partner asks Randy, a law clerk, to prepare a memo about the current Internal Revenue Code. The partner wants new additions to the Code included in a memo. Tom needs the information in 24 hours to prepare for a meeting with the clients. The bad news for Randy is that the Internal Revenue Code has changed quite a bit since the partner last looked at it.

Tax research, IRS code.

Obstacles and time factor: 24-hour deadline.

Information needed: Changes to the Tax Code.

Records needed: Sections of the IRS Code, comprehensive financial records produced by the clients.

Results required: Memo to partner and inserted sections of the U.S. Code.

Issues

How to handle an audit when the IRS owes money to the person(s) being audited.

Issues and Search Terms

Issue	Case Law	Statutes
Tax code and overpayment		
Audit and IRS		

Research Path: URL Tracking

<http://www.law.cornell.edu/index.html>

<http://wwwsecure.law.cornell.edu/topics/topic2.html>

<http://wwwsecure.law.cornell.edu/topics/income_tax.html>

<http://www4.law.cornell.edu/uscode/26/
index.text.html>

Search page appears for typing in search terms and
Boolean operators.

Research Method and Query Formulation

Traditional print research would mean feeding
quarters into a parking meter at the law library;
making copies; then cutting, pasting, and arrang-
ing. This is neither fun nor an effective, efficient
use of time. Randy also knows the reaction he
would get from the legal secretary who would
have to retype what looks like a mosaic art project.
Therefore, Randy might have decided, without
even asking, to type it himself.

Computer-assisted legal research changed all
that. Today, researchers enjoy many options for
legal research. For a limited number of projects, the
researcher can gather all the background information using the Internet. Increasingly, more projects
can be completed fully with the use of the Internet
and a word-processing package. After looking up a
document online, a researcher prints it right there
on a local computer, or downloads it to a disk.
Also, West Publishing offers cases on CD-ROM to
be searched at leisure without incurring per-minute
online charges.

Let us say that Randy has a personal computer,
Microsoft Word, and an Internet connection with
a browser like Netscape. Tom, the partner, asks
Randy to complete the project in 24 hours. Randy
has finished his other projects for the day. It is
about 3:30 in the afternoon. The Internet research
station in the firm library is available.

Randy logs in to the Internet, giving his name
and password. He fills out a firm sheet for time
spent on the project. The Internet connection costs
$25 per month for unlimited access. Thus, the
monthly expense is billed as overhead. No other
per-minute charges apply.

He has several options. Cornell Legal Information Institute (<http://www.law.cornell.edu/index.html>) and the Virtual Law Library (<http://www.law.indiana.edu/v-lib>) lead directly to starting points for tax research. Randy decides on the Cornell site, which has a link titled "Constitutions and Codes." Selecting this link pulls up a list of choices. He selects the U.S. Code from that list. He also has the option to select the link "Law about." Next, he finds the link titled "Income Tax" and pulls it up on the screen. There, under "Menu of sources" material, he sees the entry:

U.S. Code: 26 U.S.C.-Internal Revenue Code

He clicks on it and it leads to the index for Title 26. Lower on the page is the entry:

U.S. Supreme Court—Recent Income Tax Decisions

Randy goes on to research Title 26 of the United States Code. With the entire code available online, he scans to find added sections of the statute. While on the screen he wants, using Netscape, he pulls down the menu bar at the top of the screen. He drags the mouse down to the "save as" option. As he selects this option, the dialog box pops up for options to save. He decides to save the information on a Zip disc so he can keep his hard drive from getting too crowded with documents. He switches back into the Word document, which includes a memo header to present to the partner. After typing a small summary, he alt/tabs back to the File Manager. He clicks on the saved IRS Code file. He opens it, then selects the information to appear in the memo by clicking on and highlighting the text. Then he chooses the Copy function in the Edit menu. This allows him to lift a copied form of this file, in this case a memo to the supervising attorney. He chooses "paste" from the menu options (or he can press the Control (CTRL) key and the V key to paste). The required information is then poured into the document prepared for the attorney.

Randy highlights the added text and chooses for it to be in italics and bold. Transferring the text and making the font different takes a few minutes. He then prepares the memo for printing, setting up the margins and other format features, still using the word-processing program.

After he edits his added comments, he decides to click on the option:

Supreme Court: Recent Income Tax Decisions ·

and finds several cases challenging a new provision. He writes a brief summary of the cases. Finally, the memo is ready for presentation. It's about 4:45. The law clerk logs in his time for researching and writing onto the firm time sheet forms. The total savings can be measured in terms of low-cost online time, no trips to the law library, and no photocopying. He successfully integrated the necessary Code provisions into his memo.

Task #2: Environmental Law

Incident

A firm represents a company that has been charged with violating the Clean Air Act.

Assignment

The memo and file attachments must be sent from a branch office in Houston to an office in Dallas. The partner, Katherine, asks Melanie, an associate, to gather and send the documents by Friday for a hearing the next week.

Research and prepare a memo regarding the Clean Air Act (CAA), 42 U.S.C. ch. 85.

Obstacles and time factors: None.

Information needed: 42 U.S.C. ch. 85.

Results required: Summary of the CAA.

Issues

How to conduct environmental research.

Issues and Search Terms

Issue	Case Law	Statutes
Clean Air Act and violation		
Emission standards		

Research Path: URL Tracking

<http://www.law.cornell.edu>

<http://www.law.cornell.edu/index.html>

<http://wwwsecure.law.cornell.edu/topics/
topic2.html>

<http://wwwsecure.law.cornell.edu/topics/
environmental.html>

Research Method and Query Formulation

This research problem involves gathering statutes for a memo regarding environmental law. Melanie uses the firm's Internet connection and links up to Cornell at <http://www.law.cornell. edu>.

Melanie uses the Cornell site's drop-down menu titled "Law about" to locate environmental law resources. She finds the needed chapter—42 U.S.C. ch. 85, Clean Air Act—through the Legal Information Institute offered through Cornell Law School. Once she clicks on the link to the CAA, she uses the "save as" menu to save the text onto a disk. She finds the corresponding Code of Federal Regulations provisions listed below. The memo to be written must include a summary of several provisions of the statute and two C.F.R. sections.

After saving each statutory and C.F.R. section as separate text files, Melanie pours the text into a document created in her word processor; this document will become the memo. After reading documents presented by the client to the partner, she begins to shape up the memo. To be sure the provisions are the latest and to gather case references, Melanie shepardizes the provisions using print versions of the citators. She summarizes relevant information. Several hours later, the memo is ready to send.

Melanie sends the memo via email with the research as a file attachment. The receiving party, Kyle, an associate in the branch office, receives the message within a few seconds. He prints out the memo and delivers an extra copy to Katherine and another partner, Roy, who is also working on the case.

This research project saved time and money in several ways:

1. No overnight delivery service was required.
2. No long-distance telephone calls were needed; the memo sender (in Houston) only called a local Internet provider to get the material to the receiver in Dallas.
3. No extra copies had to be made by the sender; an electronic backup was saved on a disk (taking up only a minute amount of space).
4. No physical cutting and pasting was required—just online cropping, segmenting, and formatting.
5. No trips to the law library were required, no parking fees were paid, and no photocopying charges were incurred.

Electronic research and document assembly are faster, more efficient, and much more legible than traditional research. Hacking one's way through stacks of papers at the last minute means sure disaster and frustration. Certainly, frustrations will be encountered in trying to use only electronic resources to fully prepare a document (e.g., slow Internet connections, frequent disconnections, and time spent learning to use search engines and navigate research sites). But the learning curve will soon pay off in time savings, freedom, flexibility, and options for legal research.

Task #3: Criminal Law

Incident

A client, Russell, faces trial on a charge of driving while intoxicated (DWI).

Assignment

The supervising attorney, Troy, asks his paralegal, Rhonda, to research the statutes that specify the elements of a DWI charge. Troy wants to devise a strategy whereby the client can fight the charge as inaccurate or unreliable.

Prepare a memo regarding DWI representation, including a careful analysis of the strengths and weaknesses of this client's case.

Obstacles and time factor: One week.

Information needed: Texas state law on DWI.

Results required: Comprehensive statement on DWI issues facing the client and affecting the ability to fight the charge.

Issues

Elements of the DWI charge as set out in Texas state law, and statutorily prescribed penalties and punishments for DWI.

Issues and Search Terms

Issues	Case Law	Statutes
DWI and DUI		
Driving while intoxicated		
Drunk driving		

Research Path: URL Tracking

Cop Shop

<http://www.cowtown.net/Cop_Shop>

<http://www.cowtown.net/Cop_Shop/
texaslaw.html>

<http://www.cowtown.net/Cop_Shop/
pcindex.html>

<http://www.cowtown.net/Cop_Shop/
penal_code_index.html>

Crimelynx

<http://www.crimelynx.com>

<http://www.crimelynx.com/research.html>

Research Method and Query Formulation

Whether she knows it initially or not, Rhonda needs to find the Texas Penal Code. To begin the search, she locates the Virtual Law Library (<http://wwwlaw.indiana.edu/v-lib>). She scrolls down to "state." She locates state laws concerning DWI. She finds the following references:

Texas Penal Code

Section 49.04 Driving While Intoxicated

Punishment V.T.C.A. Penal Code Section 12.22

Cross references:
V.T.C.A. Alcoholic Beverage Code;
Section 1.04

Community Supervision, Deferred
Adjudication 42.12

Public Place, V.T.C.A. Penal Code
Section 1.07

Rhonda decides to look up other sites through
which to access the Texas Penal Code, to add to
these bookmarks. She finds the Code through a
Webcrawler search using the phrase "Texas Penal
Code". She clicks on one of the references from this
search result list. On this site, Cop Shop (<http://
www.cowtown.net/Cop_Shop>), she finds provisions of the Texas Penal Code and saves them to a
disk for Troy. As she is searching, she also finds
Crimelynx (<http://www.crimelynx.com>), a legal
resource center for criminal defense practitioners.
It gives her yet another option to search state and
federal sites for criminal law resources.

Task #4: Legislative Research

Incident

A client wants information about the history of
recent legislation.

Assignment

Tommy, a law clerk, is asked by a firm partner,
Angel, to conduct a legislative history search. He
must find all relevant material from slip laws,
the United States Statutes at Large, *United States
Congressional and Administrative News,* the *Digest of
Public General Bills and Resolutions,* the *Congressio-
nal Record,* the *Congressional Index,* House and
Senate calendars, and House and Senate journals.

Obstacles and time factor: Two weeks.

Information needed: Legislative history.

Records needed: Slip laws and House/Senate calendars.

Results required: Comprehensive legislative history.

Issues

What is the complete legislative history for a particular piece of legislation.

Issues and Search Terms

Issues	Case Law	Statutes
Legislative history		
Internet resources on legislative histories		

Research Path: URL Tracking

<http://thomas.loc.gov>

<http://www.house.gov>

<http://thomas.loc.gov/cp106/cp106query. html>

Research Method and Query Formulation

This is the first time Tommy has done a legislative history search. Through an Internet directory, he finds an address for the United States House of Representatives: <http://www.house.gov/>.

First, Tommy wants to read information about the legislative process in general. After reading some of the information at the THOMAS site, he decides to explore the links on the House of Representatives home page. Links include:

House Operations

House Directory

Member Offices

Committee Offices

Leadership Offices

The Legislative Process

Employment Opportunities

Through the House of Representatives site, a researcher can also click on a link to THOMAS (**<http://thomas.loc.gov>**) and directly link to the United States Code. If a researcher wants to, there is an option to write a letter to a representative.

The site provides access to:

Text of resolutions and bills considered by Congress

House floor debate information

House floor and committee action summaries and schedules

Email addresses, telephone numbers, names, and addresses of members and committees

The Declaration of Independence, the United States Constitution, and "How Laws are Made"

Capitol Hill maps and Capitol touring information

United States Code—searchable, full-text

Code of Federal Regulations

House Ethics Manual, House Rules, organization and operations information citizen feedback.

Task #5: Federal Circuit Research

Incident

A partner who is in trial on a case thinks that a very recent Second Circuit decision may affect that case. She wants to read the entire opinion so that she can decide whether the holding supports or undercuts her theory of her own case.

Assignment

A partner, Chris, asks a law clerk, James, to locate a Federal Circuit Web site that she has heard of through colleagues. She wants to find a case decided in the Second Circuit.

Obstacles and time factor: Need is immediate.

Information needed: Second Circuit opinion.

Records needed: Opinion text and any available annotations.

Results required: Full text of opinion and comprehensive analysis of the opinion.

Issues

Retrieval and analysis of a court's opinion, with presentation appropriate for partner.

Issues and Search Terms

Issues	Case Law	Statutes
Federal Circuit		
Federal cases		
Second Circuit decisions		

Research Path: URL Tracking

<http://www.law.emory.edu/LAW/law.html>

<http://www.law.emory.edu/FEDCTS>

<http://www.tourolaw.edu/2ndCircuit/main.html>

<http://www.tourolaw.edu/Excite/AT-2ndCircuitQuery.html>

<http://www.tourolaw.edu/2ndCircuit>

Research Method and Query Formulation

Luckily, James knows right where to go. He opens the site for Emory University Law School.

On their Web page, James finds a map of the United States with embedded links to various Web sites for circuit courts. If he clicks on any state, the link sends him directly to the circuit court Web sites.

In summary:

1. James opens the Emory Law site, <http://www.law.emory.edu>.
2. He selects the Second Circuit court on the map.
3. He clicks on "Law Links," <http://www.law.emory.edu/LAW/law.html>.
4. He selects the search option for locating a court decision. A user can search by party name, docket number, decision date, and/or keyword. James locates the case in the list, then clicks on the option to view and print the document as a text file.

Task #6: Locating Individuals for Referrals

Incident

A client of a law firm that does estate and tax planning asks for assistance in a products liability case. The law firm wants to refer this client to another attorney who specializes in the products liability field.

Assignment

A firm partner, Andy, asks a legal assistant, Steve, to find information about a law school colleague and where he might be located now.

Locating attorney referral sites.

Obstacles and time factor: One week.

Information needed: Contact information for a colleague.

Records needed: Printout or email of address(es) and telephone number(s).

Results required: Accurate referral information, with delivery to client as soon as possible.

Issues

What is the quickest way to locate another attorney for referral?

Issues and Search Terms

Issues	Case Law	Statutes
Products liability		
Referrals		
Alumni sites		

Research Path: URL Tracking

Steve has several options for locating legal professionals including:

- Legal Information Institute, Cornell Law School:
  <http://www.law.cornell.edu/directories.html>
- Lawoffice.com from West Legal Directory:
  <http://lawoffice.com>
- Martindale-Hubbell Lawyer Locator:
  <http://www.martindale.com/locator/home.html>
- lawyers.com:
  <http://www.lawyers.com>

Research Method and Query Formulation

Lawoffice.com from West Legal Directory (<http://lawoffice.com>) maintains information about law firms, state and federal attorneys,

and corporate counsel, including biographical
information:

> name
> firm/agency
> office address
> telephone number
> current position
> court and bar admissions and years
> areas of practice
> date and place of birth
> educational background
> current/past affiliations
> offices held

Task #7: Locating Individuals

Incident

A law firm involved in a criminal trial needs to
find a named witness to the crime.

Assignment

A firm associate, Kevin, is assigned to find the
named witness. Kevin decides, before hiring an
investigator, to try some of the "people finders"
available through the World Wide Web.

> Obstacles and time factor: As soon as possible.
> Information needed: Contact information for
> witness.
> Records needed: Telephone number and
> address.
> Results required: Information that leads the
> firm to the witness.

Issues

Locate the current whereabouts and contact information for a particular person; verify that the person located is the one needed.

Issues and Search Terms

Issues	Case Law	Statutes
People finding		
Location		
Tracer		
Tracker		

Research Path: URL Tracking

<http://people.yahoo.com>
<http://www.whowhere.lycos.com>
<http://www.iaf.net>
<http://www.who-me.com>

Research Method and Query Formulation

Many leads have led nowhere, and the Internet search is the firm's last resort before hiring a professional (and expensive) investigator. People finders provide information for legal researchers, biographers, and other professionals seeking public information. Leading people finders currently available are:

1. Yahoo! People Search: <http://people.yahoo. com> (free access)
2. Whowhere? ... the way to find people on the Web: <http://www.whowhere.lycos.com> (free access)
3. Internet @ddress finders: <http://www.iaf. net> (free access)

4. Who? Me?: <http://www.who-me.com> (free access)

5. Internet Department of Motor Vehicles: <http://www.ameri.com/dmv.dmv.htm> (paid service)

These are general starting points for finding information about individuals. The American Information Network also provides public information: <http://www.ameri.com/sherlock/sherlock. htm>. This page provides a starting point for reaching federal, state, and county criminal records. The database also includes credit reports, professional license records, education verifications, worker's compensation records, and consumer public filings (including bankruptcies, tax liens, and judgments).

In summary:

1. The associate pulls up a list of links to "People finders"

2. He searches each link for contact and background information about the person he wishes to locate.

Task #8: Criminal Law

Incident

Two police officers, who are in a public area known for drug trafficking, see a suspected drug dealer. Upon seeing the officers, the suspect runs through a nearby tavern, throwing a matchbox down on the bar as he exits. The officers inspect the matchbox, which turns out to contain cocaine, and attempt to pursue and arrest the suspected dealer.

Assignment

Bill, the firm's paralegal, is asked to research several issues for Carol, the supervising attorney.

Carol wants as much online information as possible before she begins formulating her memo to the partner in charge of this case. She will be traveling to a small town that has no law library. However, she has her laptop and from her hotel room, she will be able to use the phone jack to dial in to her Internet provider (via an 800 number). This will save her time and will help her to be prepared upon returning to the office.

> Locate criminal case law and statutes regarding abandoned property and probable cause
>
> Obstacles and time factor: Three days.
>
> Information needed: Information about abandoned property and police ability to inspect property.
>
> Records needed: Case law and law journal articles.
>
> Results required: Email synopsis of research findings and attachment of materials found.

Issues

What is the relevant case law regarding abandoned property and probable cause? Were the police officers correct in treating the matchbox as abandoned property? Did they have the right to inspect it and then arrest the suspect?

Issues and Search Terms

Issue	Case Law	Statutes
Abandoned property		
Probable cause		

Research Path: URL Tracking

Locate and retain a list of Web site Uniform Resource Locators (URLs) regarding abandoned property and probable cause. Web sites may include case law, statutes, or law review materials.

Keep a research record by cutting and pasting
relevant URLs into a table such as the following:

Web site address (URL)	Action taken	Results
\<http://www.google.com/ unclesam>	Random search for documents, listservs, and news items relating to probable cause	Numerous Web sites leading to articles and links to research sites
\<http://www.yahoo.com>	Random search for documents, listservs, and news items relating to probable cause	Article that discussed principles of probable cause in relation to case involving a traffic stop
\<http://www.law.cornell.edu/> \<http://www.law.cornell. edu/topics/topic2. html#criminal justice> \<http://www.law.cornell. edu/topics/criminal.html> \<http://www.law.cornell.edu/ constitution.billofrights. html#amendmentiv> \<http://www.law.cornell.edu/ topics/state_statutes. html#criminal_code> \<http://capitol.tlc.state.tx.us/ statutes/petoc.html> \<http://www.cowtown.com/ Cop_Shop> \<http://www.cowtown.net/ Cop_Shop/chapter_38. html#38.04>	Controlled search for information categorized by area of law and by state	

Research Method and Query Formulation

Bill begins his research via Yahoo by typing "probable cause" in the search term text box. He pulls up a list of sites, some of which appear to be relevant, others not. Bill browses the short descriptions to see which ones he should investigate further. He scrolls down the Web page to see a Supreme Court case regarding probable cause. Bill clicks on the link, hoping it will give him a good lead to other materials. He finds a news brief about probable cause in reference to searching a vehicle during a traffic stop. A United Press International and AP wire are cited, along with the docket number to the Iowa case that went to the Supreme Court. Bill decides to look further. If he finds nothing else online, he can use this case later to shepardize via WESTLAW to pull up other relevant U.S. Supreme Court and Texas cases and statutes.

Task #9: Antitrust

Incident

A state office employee, Karen, witnesses an illegal bidding procedure taking place at a state agency. She reports the incident to federal authorities, believing it to be a violation of the Sherman Act. The state agency terminates Karen's employment and the overseeing agency does nothing to investigate. She contacts an attorney to determine her right to sue. In the meantime, a company that was not allowed to bid is preparing to sue the state agency and wants to call Karen as a witness.

Assignment

Research the Sherman Act and law reviews and discussions regarding sovereign immunity.

Obstacles and time factor: One month.

Information needed: Statutes, regulations, and other information about antitrust and bidding on government contracts.

Records needed: Examples of bidding procedures; statutes and agency regulations regarding bidding procedures; case law and commentary on antitrust application to government entities.

Results required: Records on bidding with a government agency.

Issues

Does a state agency have sovereign immunity in the case of a bidding violation?

Issues and Search Terms

Issue	Case Law	Statutes
Termination of employment		
Sherman Act violation		
Sovereign immunity		
State bidding		

Research Path: URL Tracking

Indiana Virtual Law Library,
<http://www.law.indiana.edu/v-lib/>

Select the drop-down box for "Labor and Employment Law"

OR

Search by keywords

Emory Law School, for employment law issues:
<http://www.law.emory.edu/LAW/law.html>
<http://www.law.emory.edu/LAW/refdesk/toc.html>

<http://www.law.emory.edu/LAW/refdesk/
subject>

<http://www.law.emory.edu/LAW/refdesk/
subject/employ.html>

For antitrust issues:

<http://www.law.emory.edu/LAW/refdesk/
subject/sec.html>

Cornell Law,

<http://www.law.cornell.edu/topical.html>

<http://www.law.cornell.edu/topics/topic2.
html#governmental organization>

Research Method and Query Formulation

Russell, the representing firm's paralegal, is assigned to research violations of the Sherman Act and how it applies to state agencies. In addition, the paralegal needs to research sovereign immunity, as this may affect the discharged employee's ability to sue.

Task #10: Entrapment

Incident

A prison inmate is given a marked $100 bill and is encouraged to get a correctional officer to bring him contraband. When he does so, he is charged with attempted bribery. Ralph, the inmate, sues, claiming entrapment.

Assignment

Wendy, Andy's law clerk, is assigned to research all angles of this client's case.

Research the elements of entrapment and application in a prison setting.

Obstacles and time factor: Two weeks.

Information needed: Prisoners' rights information.

Records needed: Cases and law review articles.

Results required: Memorandum to supervising attorney summarizing information found online about entrapment.

Issues

Do the facts of this situation constitute entrapment?

Issues and Search Terms

Issues	Case Law	Statutes
Entrapment		
Contraband and prison		

Research Path: URL Tracking

<http://www.law.cornell.edu/topical.html>

<http://www.law.cornell.edu/topics/civil_rights.html>

<http://www.law.cornell.edu/topics/prisoners_rights.html>

Several search options are available regarding prisoners and prisoners' rights.

Research Method and Query Formulation

Andy gives Wendy the following search terms to start her research:

entrapment

inmate or prisoner and entrapment

correctional officer and entrapment

contraband and prison
correctional officer and contraband

Task #11: Privacy Law

Incident

Palmer suspects that his mother is being abused in the nursing home where she resides. He wants to install a hidden camera in her room to observe attendants and visitors. He is concerned about being sued for violation of privacy, but wonders if employees waive the right to privacy when they are in the workplace. He also fears that he could be sued by the nursing home, which would not want its possible liability captured on a videotape that could end up on news broadcasts. Palmer, who is determined to set up the camera, wants to consult with an attorney to find out the worst-case scenario should his activity be exposed. He knows he will be advised to let the authorities handle it, but he is determined to collect evidence to build his own case against the nursing home.

Assignment

Research issues of workplace privacy and elder abuse.

Obstacles and time factor: One week.

Information needed: Statutes, case law, and law review articles.

Records needed: Similar case is preferred.

Results required: Statement about workplace privacy as interpreted by the courts.

Issues

What liabilities might an individual incur if he installs a surveillance camera in his mother's private room in a nursing home?

Issues and Search Terms

Issue	Case Law	Statutes
Workplace privacy		
Videotaping and workplace surveillance		
Nursing home and resident abuse		

Research Path: URL Tracking

<http://www.law.cornell.edu/>

<http://www.law.cornell.edu/topical.html>

<http://www.law.cornell.edu/topics/topic2.
html#constitutional_law>

<http://www.law.cornell.edu/topics/topic2.
html#employment_law>

<http://www.law.cornell.edu/topics/
employment.html>

<http://www.dol.gov/>

<http://www.dol.gov/dol/public/foia/main.
htm>

<http://www.dol.gov/dol/public/foia/privlink.
htm>

·<http://www.dol.gov/cgi-bin/leave-dol.
pl?The_Department_of_Justice~http://www
.usdoj.gov/foia/ovr_indirect.htm>

Case law discussion:

<http://www.usdoj.gov/04foia/1974def-b.
htm>

Task #12: Worker's Compensation

Incident

Randall experienced back problems after an auto accident he had in 1990. In 1999, he began working for an Internet startup company. Because the staff was lean, all employees helped when computer monitors and towers had to be moved or carried in or out. The company also stocked a small break room with cases of beverages.

Randall never mentioned his previous back injury to his employer, and felt that the treatment subsequent to the injury had been adequate, though he still experienced dull pain frequently.

Several months after he began working at the Internet company, he attempted to move a system from one cubicle to another. He tripped on a cord, though he did not fall. His back was injured as a result, but his employer admitted no responsibility for the injuries, which required substantial medical care and treatment.

Randall is suing for worker's compensation benefits. He claims that his employer asked him to move the system, though no other employees were present and thus no witnesses can back up his assertion. His employer claims that Randall was trying to steal the computer system and was therefore not covered under worker's compensation.

Assignment

Research statutory, administrative, and case law to determine if Randall is eligible for worker's compensation.

Obstacles and time factor: Two months.

Information needed: Case law on worker's compensation and employee theft.

Records needed: Texts of cases and worker's compensation regulations.

Results required: Memorandum summarizing the information found.

Issues

Is an employee entitled to worker's compensation when a condition existed prior to an accident? When that employer denies responsibility and claims that the worker was not acting within the scope of his employment?

Issues and Search Terms

Issue	Case Law	Statutes
Worker's compensation		
Theft by employee		
Workplace injury		

Research Path: URL Tracking

<http://www.law.cornell.edu/>

<http://www.law.cornell.edu/topics/topic2. html#accident_and_injury>

<http://www.law.cornell.edu/topics/ workers_compensation.html>

Research Method and Query Formulation

Using broad terms, then narrower terms, the paralegal locates several law review articles about similar cases.

Task #13: Patent Law

Incident

Roger invents a tool for use in an automobile. He wants to see if he can patent it and if he is entitled to full rights to the patent for himself (not his employer, a university).

Assignment

Research patent law and the status of a university employer.

Obstacles and time factor: Two months.

Information needed: Patent laws and interpretations.

Records needed: Relevant provisions from patent laws and case law.

Results required: Information for nonattorney client.

Issues

Is an inventor entitled to a patent in his own right when he used university resources to research and produce the invention?

Issues and Search Terms

Issue	Case Law	Statutes
Patentability		
Novel, useful, not obvious		
Patent entitlement		
University research, patents		

Research Path: URL Tracking

<http://www.law.cornell.edu/>

<http://www.law.cornell.edu/topics/topic2.html#intellectual_property>

<http://www.law.cornell.edu/topics/patent.html>

<http://www.law.cornell.edu/uscode/35/pll.
   html>

<http://www.law.cornell.edu/uscode/35/ch10.
   html>

<http://www.law.cornell.edu/uscode/35/102.
   html>

Research Method and Query Formulation

Roger started with the most relevant Web sites and also did random searching to pick up any discussions in newsgroups that might bear on this question.

Task #14: Software Patent

Incident

Bill, a software developer, wants to obtain a patent, but he is concerned that his ideas have been taken by someone else who will apply for a patent first.

Assignment

Research patentability.

Obstacles and time factor: Three days.

Information needed: General information about applying for a patent.

Records needed: Patent law and regulations; patent application forms and regulations.

Results required: Enough information to make a determination if Bill has a case and should contact an attorney.

Issues

Patent entitlement and eligibility.

Issues and Search Terms

Issue	Case Law	Statutes
Patentability		
Novel, useful, not obvious		
Patent entitlement		

Research Path: URL Tracking

<http://www.law.cornell.edu/>

<http://www.law.cornell.edu/topics/topic2. html#intellectual_property>

<http://www.law.cornell.edu/topics/patent. html>

<http://www.law.cornell.edu/uscode.35/pll. html>

<http://www.law.cornell.edu/uscode.35/ch10. html>

<http://www.law.cornell.edu/uscode.35/102. html>

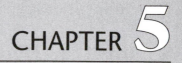

Additional Resources on the Internet

Chapter Outline

■ Virtual Law Libraries

Indiana University

The Virtual Law Library of Indiana University, discussed earlier in the text, maintains a link for searching using search terms. A drop-down list for searching by topic or type includes:

Administrative law

Business and commercial law

Civil and appellate procedure

Constitutional law

Contracts

Criminal law and evidence

Environmental law

Family law

Foreign and international law

Intellectual property

Labor and employment law

Property law

Taxation

Torts

The site also provides a gateway to other search tools and comprehensive sites.

Cornell University

Cornell University Law School Library (<http://www.lawschool.cornell.edu/lawlibrary/>) provides an excellent starting point for legal research. Links lead to legal journals and legal research sites.

■ Law Schools Online

Following are some of the law schools online:

Baylor University
<http://law.baylor.edu/default.htm>

Case Western Reserve University
<http://holmes.law.cwru.edu>

Constitutional Educational Research
Foundation—Paralegal Self-Study Courses
<http://calparalegal.com>

Drake University
<http://www.law.drake.edu/>

Duke University
<http://www.law.duke.edu>

Duquesne University
<http://www.duq.edu/law/law.html>

Emory University
<http://www.law.emory.edu>

Florida State University
<http://www.law.fsu.edu/>

Franklin Pierce Law Center
<http://www.fplc.edu>

Georgetown University
<http://www.ll.georgetown.edu>

Georgia State University
<http://law.gsu.edu/>

Gonzaga University
<http://law.wuacc.edu/gonzaga/libhome.
html>

Illinois Institute of Technology—Chicago Kent College of Law
<http://www.kentlaw.edu>

Indiana University–Bloomington
<http://www.law.indiana.edu>

Indiana University–Indianapolis
<http://www.iulaw.indy.indiana.edu/>

John Marshall Law School
<http://www.jmls.edu/>

Ohio Northern University—Petit College of Law
<http://www.law.onu.edu/>

Pepperdine University
<http://law-www.pepperdine.edu/>

Regent University at Queen's University
<http://qsilver.queensu.ca/law/>

Rutgers University—Camden
<http://www-camlaw.rutgers.edu/>

Saint Louis University
<http://law.slu.edu/>

Santa Clara University
<http://www.scu.edu/law/>

Seattle University
<http://www.law.seattleu.edu/>

Seton Hall University
<http://law.shu.edu/>

Stanford University
<http://lawschool.stanford.edu/>

Syracuse University
<http://www.law.syr.edu/>

Temple University
<http://www.temple.edu/lawschool/>

Touro College—Jacob D. Fuchsberg Law Center
<http://www.tourolaw.edu/>

Tufts University—Fletcher School of Law & Diplomacy
<http://fletcher.tufts.edu/>

Tulane University
<http://www.law.tulane.edu/>

University of Alberta
<http://www.law.ualberta.ca/>

University of Arizona
<http://www.law.arizona.edu/>

University of Arkansas—Fayetteville
<http://law.uark.edu/>

University of British Columbia
<http://flair.law.ubc.ca/>

University of California–Hastings
<http://www.uchastings.edu>

University of Chicago
<http://www.law.uchicago.edu/>

University of Cincinnati
<http://www.law.uc.edu/>

University of Colorado
<http://stripe.colorado.edu/
~lawadmin/>

University of Connecticut
<http://www.law.uconn.edu/>

University of Idaho
<http://www.uidaho.edu/law/>

University of Illinois
<http://www.law.uiuc.edu/>

University of Kansas
<http://www.law.ukans.edu/>

University of Kentucky
<http://www.uky.edu/law/>

University of Louisville
<http://www.louisville.edu/law/>

University of Michigan
<http://www.law.umich.edu/>

University of Mississippi
<http://www.olemiss.edu/depts/
law_school/law-hom.html>

University of Missouri at Columbia
<http://www.law.missouri.edu/>

University of North Dakota
<http://www.law.und.nodak.edu/>

University of Oklahoma
<http://www.law.ou.edu/>

University of Oregon
<http://www.law.uoregon.edu/>

University of Pennsylvania
<http://www.law.upenn.edu/>

University of Pittsburgh
<http://jurist.law.pitt.edu/index.htm>

University of San Diego
<http://www.acusd.edu/usdlaw/>

University of Southern California
<http://www.usc.edu/dept/law-lib/>

University of Texas at Austin
   <http://www.law.utexas.edu/>

University of Tulsa
   <http://www.utulsa.edu/law/>

University of Washington
   <http://www.law.washington.edu/>

Villanova University
   <http://vls.law.villanova.edu/>

Washburn University
   <http://lawlib.wuacc.edu/>

Washington University
   <http://www.wulaw.wustl.edu/>

Wayne State University
   <http://www.law.wayne.edu/>

■ Electronic Law Journals

Many legal journals are available on the World
Wide Web, including the following:

Cornell Law Review
   <http://www.lawschool.cornell.edu/clr>

*E Law—Murdoch University Electronic Journal
of Law*
   <http://www.murdoch.edu.au/elaw/>

Federal Communications Law Journal
   <http://www.law.indiana.edu/fclj/fclj.html>

Florida Law Weekly
   <http://www.polaris.net/~flw/flw.htm>

Florida State University Law Review
   <http://www.law.fsu.edu/journals/index.
   html>

Global Legal Studies Journal
<http://www.law.indiana.edu/glsj/glsj.html>

Law News Network.com
<http://www.lawnewsnetwork.com/>

Law Technology Product News
<http://www.ljextra.com/ltpn/>

Michigan State University Journal of International Law and Practice
<http://www.dcl.edu/jil/index.html>

National Association of Forensic Economics Journal
<http://nafe.net>

New York Law Journal
<http://www.ljx.com/NYLJ0809.html>

Richmond Journal of Law and Technology
<http://www.urich.edu/~jolt/>

Stanford Journal of International Law
<http://www-leland.stanford.edu/group/SJIL/index.html>

Stanford Journal of Law, Business and Finance
<http://www.stanford.edu/group/sjlbf/>

Texas Intellectual Property Law Journal
<http://www.utexas.edu/law/journals/tiplj/index.html>

Transportation Law Journal
<http://www.du.edu/~transplj/>

Villanova Publications
<http://vls.law.vill.edu/pubs/>

Villanova University School of Law: The Internet Legal Research Compass
<http://vls.law.vill.edu/compass/>

Washington Law Review
<http://www.law.washington.edu/~wlr/>

Web Journal of Current Legal Issues
<http://webjcli.ncl.ac.uk/>

▓ Researching Law Directories

Law directories available via the Internet provide helpful information for making referrals or looking up an attorney. The most commonly used directories are the Martindale-Hubbell Lawyer Locator (<http://www.martindale.com/locator/home.html>); lawyers.com; and Lawoffice.com from the West Legal Directory. Other directories include those of the American Bar Association, Online Section Directory (ABA membership required); and the International Bar Association (membership required). Martindale-Hubbell gives the following information for each attorney listed: date of birth, date of admission to bar, specialty, American Bar Association membership, college degrees, and law school attended. West's Legal Directory includes law firm information and short individual biographies. FindLaw (<http://www.findlaw.com/l4firms/index.html> and <http://www.findlaw.com/l4firms/search. html>) also provides links to directories of attorneys and biographical information.

Index

C

Securities and Exchange Commission, 41
Session laws, 9
Shears, Toni, 16
Shepardizing, 50, 64
Shepard's Citations, 14–15
Sherman Act, 64
Slip laws, 10, 53
Software, patenting, 73–74
Sovereign immunity, 64–66
Spelling, xi, 27
State law, 52–53
Statsky, William, 23
Statutes, 4, 5. *See also* Law
　　locating, 3
　　publication of, 9–10
Statutes at Large, 9–10
Substantive law, 40
Supreme Court Reporter, 8
Synonyms, 23

T

Tax law, 44–48
Taxation, 18
10-K reports, 41
Terms and terminology, 22–26
Text, importing, 27
Theft, 70–71
Thesauri, 23, 26
THOMAS, 54, 55
Trade names, 18
Trademarks, 18
Traffic offenses, 51–53
Treaties, 5, 10, 42

U

Uniform resource locators (URLs), x, 62–63
United Nations, 42
United States Code, 10, 55
United States Code Annotated, 7, 10
United States Code Service, 10
United States Code Service Advance, 7
United States Congress. *See* Congress
United States Congressional and Administrative News, 53